Thor's Light

Poems by

Richard Sellwood

First Edition
1st June 2016
ISBN: 978-1-907435-32-4

Published by Dempsey & Windle

Cover Design ©Janice Windle 2016

dempseyandwindle.co.uk

Thor's Light by Richard Sellwood

Contents

Travellers' Tales

Our teacher was a traveller returned
each autumn
and I would sit waiting for her tales
of distant lands and strange folk.

The old walls of the school
painted green and cream
and the smell of carbolic soap
opened out to places where

children wore clogs and spoke
a different tongue, with blonde hair
and brightly patterned shirts,
living in white-washed farms.

I dreamt I could meet these
aliens, who from their windows
viewed canals and dykes
lined with poplar trees,

played hopscotch in the fields
gathering in the harvest
in copper autumn light,
carrying their milk from the dairy

and singing songs around the fire.
I imagined poppies blooming,
tulips swaying in the wind.
But didn't hear the icy history

beneath the furrows
the tumuli covering
the men whose names
were children of our school.

Hawthorn

Below Shippen Hill
the Hawthorn is in blossom.
My mother warned me not to bring it in the house
and told me how my grandmother scolded her
when she set them in a vase on the kitchen table,
'they smell of plague'
with a hint of Romany magic.

In Donegal, at Beltane
under balefires on smoke blue hills
beacons serve notice and maidens dance in circles
until the chosen one is snatched
by the white goddess
who holds quickthorn to her breast.

Joseph of Arimathea's pilgrim stick,
as swifts carousel the clouds,
plunged in Glastonbury Tor,
dowsing his way along ley lines
and crowning the hill in thorns.

Now the laying of hedge
by an open field in which scattered flints lie
near memorial stones, jumbled and broken
summon the word haegthorn
deep basso profundo from a Saxon warlord

and that language echoes in my boyhood
dream; touching god'swit hard bark
with herbs of spring,
climbing the barethorn,
defying the boundary,
hearing the maudlin cuckoo,
opposing enclosure and looking out across the fence
from the tree-top
into another world.

Dinner Time

Each day the dinner-line pilgrimage
to the dour Methodist Church rooms,
an orderly queue marshalled
to graffiti scrawled trestle tables
arranged like an Oxbridge hall.

Above the stage, never used,
the bearded Christ presides
over the taking of bread
and kids line up, as if for communion.

Everything seems big,
the serving-ladies' arms,
the dark stained ceiling
and the draughty corridors
hiding changing rooms
and mysterious places
we never visit.

Ritual demands Grace
with pat words intoned
in dreary ignorance.
Then the slap of mash,
a mush of peas
and curdled meat
breaks the morning fast:
chorales of clattering cutlery
counterpoint infant chatter.

Miss Pocock, head teacher,
traveller to far off lands,
a zealot of the rationing era
watches the clearing of the plates.

It is then we learn the lesson of difference,
once again we see we're not
all alike:

a wail rises like a sudden tornado
to a high crescendo,
'I'm allergic to fish, I can't eat this,
I'm allergic to fish.'

Everything seems to stop
Jesus appears to believe
it is a test
and then there is the odd bold titter.

Distraught, red-faced, the new boy
Nigel Colley, bovine headed,
only child of elderly parents,
screams again the word that
none of us have ever heard,
'Allergic.'

Horse Chestnut

Gripping tightly our sticks of yew,
(named the bone)
pulling back green-stick arms
like archers at Agincourt,
we aim at the highest conkers
survivors of the night's wrecking wind
and toss the wood into the sky
and watch the rain of glossy eyeballs
fall to earth.

Then there is a scramble,
the best child wins
grasping his prize,
polishing it against the duffle coat
his mother made him wear,
'for there is a chill in the air today.'

This matins ritual, at the lych-gate,
near a war memorial
where the dead wait
under the old horse chestnut,
as the golden harvest is gathered in
and gifts are laid in St Peter's aisle;
the boys prime their conkers,
using an alchemy of vinegar
vulcanizing them to hard nuts,
precisely skewering the bitter pith,
almost tasting the poison broth
oozing out of the gimlet-hole,

as it hardens to flinty stone
like frost on a grave.
September mist carries
an early scent of decay
as the cracking of skulls begins,
a schoolboy duel;

the battle cries are heard
across the green
as the cobblers concuss,
wood cracks
like a rap of timpani
and brothers take arms.

Pomegranate

With tales of Moses and the Exodus
Miss Smith enchanted our ears
like Scheherazade, taking us to
A mystic shore, the promised land.

Greasy street markets with vendors
trading spices, silk, herbs, citrus
bustling narrow streets and beyond,
the desert, the journey of blood.

For "we be all dead men" now;
she took the dark spirit fruit
and split it through, her penknife
glinting in russet autumn light.

A treasure trove of ruby
seeds spilled from its
pure white centre
like jewels from a pirate's chest.

In the darkness of Hades
Persephone held out this fruit
of the dead to light her way
and eat up the night and winter.

They said Djehuty, Queen Hatshepsut's
menial, held the dry seeds
to his heart, a love token
resting in his tomb
and the blazing flowers
lifted caravansarais
along the silk road
blessing the seller's perfume.

It glowed on her desk
a coral lantern
playing conjuring tricks:
the shape of a grenade.

Outbuildings

They are not for living in,
stores of tools or hay
with battered benches and oil stones
for honing old blades;

bicycle pumps, broken wheels, mouldering papers and magazines
claimed by the dank gods;
outsiders in places where the light never quite reaches
and the dark never quite leaves.

In an old coal shed at school
I rummaged in the litter left by war belaboured kids,
the treasure I found, a mildewed print,
Harold Godwinson vanquished: William the Norman,

a vagrant snarling in victory;
they come to rest
in my childhood dream:
I learnt a lesson of history,

the smell lingers and is revived
as I cross the courtyard
open the creaking door
and look into the cellar of my past.

Michaelmas

Elegylight crossed the fields
dawngolden reflecting like
stained glass on the corn.

Out of its pen
a stubble-goose
is Michael's sacrifice,

gleaning his mortality
from the seeds he pecked
just a moment past;

husks like discarded shells
in this sundying moment,
lay scattered in the yard,

picked by farm sparrows
flitting beneath eves,
watching swallows feeling

the click of their songline,
ancient callings from
winds in the desert;

massing the skies,
pilots awaiting orders
whistling tuneless songs,

scanning the ploughed
downland; mapping
old ley-lines,

passages from grave
to grave. Chaff in the
furrows: devil's spit

on the berries; out
of mist a spider's
web traps the plane,

ravelled in mesh
its guns broken antennae,
a wounded bird

marking its trail
one last time:
watching the archangel

in his line of sight,
as the sun sets,
a burnt umber blessing the land.

Rookery.

A winter field is flooded, iced
bare frost chills the air;
at the border beneath withered Elms
words are muttered in the dusk

as the February birds settle
into a dark resting at night,
their trees cloud shadowed
with a language of coldness

by a guttural croak
as if stuck in the throat.
This city of silhouetted branches
protectorate of eggs against sterile weathers,

an east wind as orange day breaks,
birds swarm black in the matins sky
charting ancestral paths over wood, field or town
speaking as if the air is a love charm.

Midwinter

Midwinter mummers'
Foul journeys
In borough roads:
Cold trade of the farmer

Sluiced in mud.

Ghosts of fog
Spike blackthorn;
A witch's wand
In absent light.

Starved by fields

Solstice tramp,
Wolfshead,
Dowses blackout
Under parish lanterns:

Fugitive tombs.

The Anglo-Saxon name for January was Wulf-monath because hungry wolves were especially active then. Witch's wands were reputedly made of Blackthorn wood. Wolfshead is an old country word for fugitives and parish lantern refers to the moon.

Scots Pine

The sun blazed red
on to rusted trunks
out of which resin pours
like blood oozing
from the flesh.

I felt through
the fissured bark;
within a body
indwelling and left
by Osiris for us to find.

A copse in the distance
dark against light
in the heather and sand;
marking points
on drover's roads.

Treading the pine
needles, feeling no pain
in a lagoon of light
pale greenish-blue, the god
rustles like wind.

Picking up the cone
he throws it
far and wide, pitched
like a cricket ball
to the furthest boundary.

Where it lands
time begins his unravelling
game, as the hard knot
breaks from its kernel
gripping the bed of soil.

And wood snaps back
springing the soft
leaves into the air
like spines of an urchin
growing sapling fast.

Red Kites

A pigeon breaks from woods
crossing water meadows and open fields.

There is a mew from the sky
as Red Kites circle high,

a ballet among rain clouds,
a dark shadow in sunlight;

birds learning scavenging
grace the motorways

earning a reputation for stealing linen
they gather like desert vultures

and send a shiver down the spine.
Driven by mass slaughter,

the spray of shotgun,
into barren exile,

they have spread wings
and spy us as if we are carrion

in an Oxford rose garden
where the water rises

and sedge warblers hum
deep within rustling reeds.

Poplars

Always the trees lining the distance
edging the horizon on the polder.
They shiver, a little, in the sea swept wind,
as if cold or living with fear.

They remember the avenues
the shaded lines of unwinding trails
echoing with the soldier's tread
and how their hearts turned charcoal;

three sisters weeping for a brother
who crossed the constellation,
black-edged like a telegram
bearing bad news

his light a Verey illuminating
the road on which he sank and died.
They still stand, a century later,
the sorrow quivering their leaves.

Last Day of November

On this last day of November
I have looked back at snow

on the bitter east wind. Out of
windows watched lashing rain

carry its dirge across the dark
valley, grey clouds shifting

their mist up the mountains.
This last day, the river's flood

surging, whirling down rocks
to fall, this end of month time,

moor grass blowing cold
before winter's plunge,

into a mirror of red, dead leaves
as late daylight sun plays

on a stand of birch trees,
leaving ghostwhite shimmering

in the sour brooding sky of
this last November day.

Badger

Rooting in the elm gaps
beneath the hedge
where it stood above the rest

I scurry with creatures much smaller
and hear the click of their tongues
in a language I no longer know.

Smelling the scent of dead rot
dampness of woodlice and slip of worm
I dig much deeper

into catacombs long
forgotten, where we are known
as "Grey" or "Brock"

silent ghosts underground
a flit of light
quicksilver shadows

finding the old routes
crossing new-laid tarmac
shuffling in derelict sites

they say we consort
with milk cows
breaking laws of kin

where once our dynasty
ruled. This ancient wisdom
has proved hopeless

against the gas they use
or the turbulent traps
that fill our living chambers.

St Michael's Crypt

Inside the Ringstrasse
Saint Michael's crypt holds secrets
for the dead are buried here
ghosts piled one on one
becoming a crunchy soil.

The lady, smartly dressed, multilingual,
guides us like Virgil leading Dante
pointing out the coffin of her
sleeping beauty, as if she were a friend,
peaceful in the dark and silence

where the funnelled air
has mummified the burgers
of Vienna: four hundred years
one man still wears his wig
and taps his shoes against the wood

keeping awake an expectant
lady, her tomb decorated
with delicate roses, symbol
of some long-forgotten love,

under the burial shafts
in candle-lit gloom
passageways for priests to follow
until under the high altar
they sleep, while burnished

sunlight glints in shafts
picking out the golden
glory above them.
And our guide, finishing her tour,

points to Metastasio
(I think again of Virgil)
and wonder if, when we are gone
back to our world,
will the crypt sing his words?

Bach's Journey

I pass down a street and hear the water beneath
like a diviner
imagining that music flows as history underground
sailing to us with the dead.

Bach on the long journey from Arnstadt
to hear Buxtehude on the Baltic coast,
in Lubeck, in dark December, play at Marienkirch
the snow mounting up, a passacaglia, winter's song,

his fugue spins eternity, the blind blizzard of faith
glimpsed in the high organ loft
among brick pillars of Lutheran cathedrals
stops and glottals, the unguided motion

on the foot-pedal.
Pleading for redemption in an Agnes Dei
and charming angels until they want to live on earth.
I turn away from the church door

in the arctic wind
and wonder where I've heard that voice before.

Stranger Lady

They thought she was a ghost
the stranger lady in the organ loft;
a girl whose eyes shone like stars,
singing her dark contralto melody,

in plainest blue with a mop cap,
her simple face watching
contrapunctal inventions,
as Bach worked by candlelight.

And if death ran in her veins
he did not see it,
the blush on her neck
the light on her wimple.

Passacaglia

Based on Britten's 'Peter Grimes'.

"Tonight, boy, I will throw you into the sea,
you will sing, boy, to the sea tonight;
moonlight will shine on your bones
and curlewhaunted sound will carry onto the strand."
Fenmist hides his curses as the fisherman returns
saying, untwist this cacophony in my mind,
compose music of this tempest
look for treasure in the deeptorn waves.

By the shelllistening waters of California,
homeyearning and reading in the paths of exile
as a stranger, the music is heard
across the space of time brought in by the sea on a sandy shore.
It seems the forties in war-torn Europe
find a badbloodbrother in Grimes
a passacaglia drawing them together
in a dance for men on a Suffolk marsh.
And the ghost sings
"tonight, boy, I will throw you to the sea
you will lament in the sea tonight."

Composition

(In Memory of Pierre Boulez)

It is not sound yet
quavering on the ear
in time which is not time

this music snatches and retreats
there is no melody
no matching of birdsong or sea wave
refusing to cluster into notes

the chorus lies beyond horizons
barely the ring of tinnitus
or church bells in some far off parish:

rumble of planes scribbling the clouds
traffic in hurried city streets
even the dark noise humming in the universe
like medieval celestial spheres,

burrowing in mines fracking the earth
storming tsunami ravaging palms
tremors antediluvian totems
nor cracking ice deep in the polar cap

the rush of water buried at earth's heart
lying undiscovered

this has not arrived
incubating and growing:
a fragment.

Mrs Andrew's Hands

(After the portrait by Thomas Gainsborough).

There is a mist
where her hands lay;
pale and delicate
veiling mystery

like a Madonna
with her child.
Wandering paths
in the morning dew,

beneath the oak,
she sits passive;
longing beyond
the portrait

and the view
for the baby
she touches, stirring
in her womb.

Virginia Woolf 's Last Testimony

'Dearest, I feel certain that I am going mad again: I feel we can't go through another of these terrible times. And I shan't recover this time.'
Virginia Woolf's last letter to Leonard Woolf, March 1941.

It sounds like the sea outside my room

the wind skids across the moors

fragments of slate break beneath the hammer

Against the window the waves throw stones

I listen for the sound of him in the corridors

feel his hand like a reptile, roaring waters in my ears

sickness is coming and the curtains are drawn

they will leave me alone: they will not visit me

I am drinking my lonely Veronal, mixed in wine which I hate

I have left the window wide open and hear the traffic below

the voices of tradesmen courting the maidservants

a dissonant song, they sing to me these sirens

and tempt me; seduce me, tender hands crawling inside my body.

I want to fledge, to defenestrate. I have thought of shell-shocked Septimus

impaled on railings and his wife crying.

They say my pulse races as if I have less time than others

More beats of the heartsong, longer the time in the coffin

and now the pulse jumps as I am filled with fears

phobias, strangers milling in my room

the crowd in the Tavistock Square peering at me

on my pale counterpane my anorexic body like a skeleton

and the words streaming from my shut mouth unable to write it down or say it

I look at myself like someone else, my eyes are stone

I count out the years as I wander to the river

a terrible cold winter, ice in my genitals.

For every year a stone. Once more I glance over my shoulder

weighing myself down

to check that I am no longer wasting your life.

The Long Mynd

Windswept wild moor
shadow on heath
where the dark raven flies
its cawharsh mocking lost
wayfarers

I remember the Reverend Carr's
Night in the Snow
a holy man searching for home

The Port Way marks
high ground and tumuli
and long dead men
who gathered heather
scraping existence in the bogs.

We look down Bilbatch
where an eagle wings the air
and marsh ponies graze
the valley etched into upland
stone.

Places, Old Lands' Wood,
The Hollows, Tump and Coates Farm,
shelters from storm and hail,
trees, bent in harmony with the wind
spring leaved and singing
alongside Darnford Brook.

Sun shines on gorse in
the Golden Valley like a river of light
running in the umber

of last year's ferns,
the call of the melancholy curlew

at the ford a few scattered rocks
and an empty farm
eyes us with hostile eyes:
here, we lose the track.

The Long Man

1

Windover hill touched
with solstice light
and the long man rises

to make his pilgrimage,
staffs in either hand
like an alpine skier

or a power walker
striding the chalk,
facing downland rain.

A lone hang-glider
catches air streams
and the long man watches,
canny and secret
guarding his turf.

2

In summer we parked
next a Mini Traveller
dubbed with peace signs.

Following the track,
cow parsley hiding
a barbed wire boundary

and furrows where
rainwater ran white and chalky,
our boots slipping

as the horizon turns angry,
migraine aura with jagged lines,
a rumbling of storm,

brown-purple clouds
crackling electricity;
we shelter the children

in a coombe, like a dug-out,
hiding in brambles
scuffed by rabbits

and the unmistakeable scent of fox.
We have companions,
a hippie woman, who hands out

nuts from blue Tupperware,
sharing her hoard
as the rain hammers.

3

thirsty chalk drinks the water
we enter the gate of night sky,
with Balder, our Saxon god
handling the lightning like a precious sword.

cutting into the rock
wraiths of the Benedictine Priory
stand affronted by pagan deities
and rub their palms with Sanicle.

then Dodman hails wayfarers
guiding pilgrims on their path
with his exact theodolite
and passing knowledge in his horns.

we hear weaving with the chattering larks,
as sunlight settles on his long loins,
a phantom song,
"Doddiman, doddiman, put out your horn,
Here comes the thief to steal your corn."

and there is a theft, I feel,
as I look at the white lines,
improved and trimmed,
reflecting Thor's light from who knows where.

Richard Sellwood was born in 1954 and became enchanted by the poems of W. B. Yeats at primary school. He studied at Cardiff, London and Sussex universities where he was able to pursue his passion for literature. After working as an economic researcher and then as a postman, he has been an English teacher for many years. His own poems are often inspired by nature and the past; he enjoys experimenting with language and form.

Richard has just completed a fantasy novel, 'The Time Talker' and 'Thor's Light' is his first collection of poems. In 2006 he co-founded The Cranleigh Writers' Group, which has regular meetings and encourages local creative talent. He is married with three daughters and lives in Ewhurst, Surrey.

www.ingramcontent.com/pod-product-compliance
Ingram Content Group UK Ltd.
Pitfield, Milton Keynes, MK11 3LW, UK
UKHW041903190726
13854UKWH00003B/1058

9 781907 435324